Baby Wolves at the Zoo

Cecelia H. Brannon

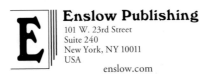

Enslow Publishing
101 W. 23rd Street
Suite 240
New York, NY 10011
USA

enslow.com

Published in 2016 by Enslow Publishing, LLC.
101 W. 23rd Street, Suite 240, New York, NY 10011

Library of Congress Cataloging-in-Publication Data

Brannon, Cecelia H.
 Baby wolves at the zoo / by Cecelia H. Brannon.
   p. cm. — (All about baby zoo animals)
 Includes bibliographical references and index.
 ISBN 978-0-7660-7164-3 (library binding)
 ISBN 978-0-7660-7162-9 (pbk.)
 ISBN 978-0-7660-7163-6 (6-pack)
 1. Wolves — Infancy — Juvenile literature. 2. Zoo animals — Juvenile literature. I. Brannon, Cecelia
H. II. Title.
 QL737.C22 B73 2016
 599.773'139—d23

Printed in the United States of America

To Our Readers: We have done our best to make sure all website addresses in this book were active and appropriate when we went to press. However, the author and the publisher have no control over and assume no liability for the material available on those websites or on any websites they may link to. Any comments or suggestions can be sent by e-mail to customerservice@enslow.com.

Photos Credits: Cover, p. 10 Critterbiz/Shutterstock.com; pp. 1, 3 (right), 8, 18 Geoffrey Kuchera/Shutterstock.com; pp. 4–5 AntoinetteW/Shutterstock.com; p. 6 © iStockphoto.com/ alexandrumagurean; pp. 12, 14, 22 Holly Kuchera/Shutterstock.com; pp. 3 (center), 16, Vibe Images/ Shutterstock.com; pp. 3 (left), 20, © iStockphoto.com/John Pitcher.

Contents

Words to Know

howl

pack

pup

Who lives at the zoo?

A baby wolf lives at the zoo!

A baby wolf is called a pup.

Wolf pups can be many colors. Their fur can be gray, brown, red, black, or even white!

A wolf pup can hear, see, and smell very well. This helps it find its mother.

Wolf pups love to play. They wrestle and chase each other. They even like to throw toys to each other!

A wolf pup lives in the zoo with its family. A family of wolves is called a pack.

A wolf pup eats kibble and raw meat and chews on bones. It gets food from the zookeeper.

A wolf pup learns to howl when it is very young. It also whines, barks, and growls. This is how it talks to other wolves and its zookeepers.

You can see a wolf pup at the zoo!

Read More

Marsh, Laura. *National Geographic Readers: Wolves*. Washington, DC: National Geographic Children's Books, 2012.

Meister, Cari. *Wolves*. Minneapolis, MN.: Jump, 2015.

Websites

International Wolf Center
www.wolf.org/learn/wild-kids/

National Geopraphic: Gray Wolf
kids.nationalgeographic.com/animals/gray-wolf/

Index

Guided Reading Level: C
Guided Reading Leveling System is based on the guidelines recommended by Fountas and Pinnell.

Word Count: 145